Harry Kane.

Some of the events described in this book are
based upon the author's imagination and are
probably not entirely accurate representations
of what actually happened.

Tales from the Pitch
Harry Kane
by Harry Coninx

Published by Raven Books
An imprint of Ransom Publishing Ltd.
Unit 7, Brocklands Farm, West Meon, Hampshire GU32 1JN, UK
**www.ransom.co.uk**

ISBN      978 180047 239 6
First published in 2022

TALES FROM THE PITCH

# HARRY KANE

HARRY CONINX

RAVEN

*For Nash, the only one of my friends*
*who's not an Arsenal fan*

# CONTENTS

# 1

## TOP OF THE CHARTS

*May 2021, King Power Stadium, Leicester, England*
*Leicester City v Tottenham Hotspur*

"How many Golden Boots have you won again?"

"Three, once this match is over with," Harry replied, looking at his team-mate Dele Alli.

As they stood in the tunnel of Leicester City's King Power Stadium, the final game of the Premier League season was upon them.

Win today, and Spurs would be in Europe next

season. But for Harry, there were more important matters to play for. He was level with Liverpool's Mohamed Salah as top goalscorer and he needed to score today to take home his third Golden Boot award.

"I'll try my best to set you up," added Heung-min Son, standing next to the pair.

"You owe me a few assists," joked Harry. He'd been setting up Son all season, including four assists in a single game back in September.

"You always score against Leicester anyway," said Dele. He was right. Harry had scored 16 goals in 15 matches against Leicester.

"Harry scores against everyone," scoffed Son.

The atmosphere inside the King Power was deafening. Following the COVID pandemic, fans were now allowed back in the stadium for the first time in over a year – and they were making themselves heard.

"It's loud, isn't it?" Dele muttered. "Why are they so worked up? I thought they'd already qualified for the Champions League."

"Where have you been, man?" Harry laughed. "They need to win today too!"

Beating Leicester wasn't going to be easy, and Liverpool and Salah were playing an easier game today, at home to Crystal Palace. Harry had asked one of the coaches to keep him updated on their match from the touchline. He wanted to know exactly what he needed to do to beat Salah.

"Don't let them get an early goal, boys!" Harry shouted, as they walked out onto the pitch. "Let's silence the fans!"

But after only 15 minutes Jamie Vardy raced through on goal, before tumbling under a soft challenge from Toby Alderweireld. After a brief VAR check, the referee pointed to the penalty spot. Vardy picked himself up and converted the spot kick.

Leicester were one-up, but Harry could still feel the nervousness amongst the Leicester players. They couldn't afford to concede.

Just before half-time, Spurs got their chance. Son's bouncing cross deflected off a Leicester defender and looped high over the players. Harry kept his eyes on the ball as it floated towards him, finding himself open in the middle of Leicester's penalty area.

He spun and let fly with a stinging right-footed volley. The ball cannoned past Schmeichel into the back of the net. He had his goal.

"I told you I'd set you up!" shouted Son, as the Spurs fans in the stadium erupted.

"That was nothing to do with you!" Harry laughed.

Half-time. 1-1. The first thing Harry did was find the coach. He needed to know who, if anybody, had scored for Liverpool.

"They're one-up, but it was Mané, not Salah," the coach told him. Harry was a goal ahead in the race for the Golden Boot, with only 45 minutes left to play.

There was still a win for Spurs to play for, but the second half got off to the worst possible start when they conceded another penalty. Once more, Vardy smashed it home, putting Leicester back in the lead.

"Come on, boys!" yelled Harry, keen to ensure the heads of his team-mates didn't drop. He knew that if they got a goal, Leicester would panic.

With 15 minutes left, Spurs got their equaliser. Kasper Schmeichel flapped desperately at a corner swerving towards him and deflected the ball into his own net.

"You're annoyed you didn't get a touch on that, aren't you?" substitute Gareth Bale chuckled, spotting the disappointment on Harry's face.

It was still 2-2 as the game approached 90 minutes, but Leicester too were pushing for a winner, leaving space in behind for Kane, Bale and Son to attack.

Receiving a long pass forward, Bale flicked the ball into Son, who turned and played in Harry. He skipped past the challenge of one defender and evaded the keeper's challenge. Harry was desperate to shoot, desperate to score his second goal, but he couldn't find a way through.

"Harry! Now!"

Bale's call drew his attention, and Harry spotted him lurking at the edge of the box. He rolled the ball back to the Welsh winger, who slammed it into the back of the net.

Spurs had the lead and the Leicester crowd were silent.

Bale added a fourth in stoppage time, sealing a massive 4-2 win for Tottenham and a place in European football next season.

But Harry wasn't thinking that far ahead. He was practically sprinting off the pitch, looking for the coach who had the news from the Liverpool game.

"Well?"

"You've done it!" replied the coach with a grin. "Number three!"

After being congratulated by his coaching staff and team-mates, a Premier League official approached Harry, handing him two trophies. Amazingly, Harry hadn't just won the Golden Boot for the third time – he'd also won the Playmaker Award for the player with the most assists in the league.

Harry accepted the trophies with thanks and posed for photos with them, but already his mind was on what was next. In just a few weeks he would be captaining England at the European Championships.

Maybe, just maybe, football was finally coming home this year.

# 2
# AIMING HIGH

*2004, Chingford Foundation School, Chingford, England*

"Grab the other post, come on!"

Harry grabbed the base of the goalpost and lifted, helping his brother raise the goal into the air, then the pair of them half-threw, half-placed the goal over the fence and onto the other side.

"Come on! Let's get round there!" his brother Charlie yelled as he raced out the gate.

The boys were lucky. Their garden backed on to Ridgeway Park in North London, and they were always keen to make the most of that. It was one thing practising penalties in your garden, but as they'd got older they'd needed more space to line up their shots.

Plus, after their kitchen window had taken a direct hit, their mum had insisted they play their football away from anything valuable.

"We've got a couple of hours before it gets too dark, I reckon," said Charlie, squinting into the setting sun. He was the older brother and Harry looked to him for advice on all things football – as well as a lot of other things that had nothing at all to do with football.

"Hey, hey!" Charlie shouted, as Harry set up the goal.

"What?"

"If I'm going in goal, then you'd better move the posts. I'm not staring into the sun as you blast shots at me!"

Harry chuckled and twisted the goal round so it was facing away from the sun. It meant that he'd have the sun in his eyes, but as it was him who'd be doing most of the shooting, he had to take the hit on this one.

Harry placed the ball on the ground, about ten yards from the goal.

"Too close!" Charlie called, marching forward and toe-poking the ball backwards. "Come on, Harry! It's a big day tomorrow. What's the point of shooting from there?"

Charlie was right. It *was* a big day tomorrow. David Beckham, captain of the England team and Manchester United legend, was coming down to Harry's school.

Because, amazingly, Beckham had also attended Chingford Foundation School when he was a kid – and it was because of Beckham that Harry had decided that he was going to become a professional footballer.

"Imagine it's the last minute against Greece!" Charlie shouted, as Harry placed the ball on the ground. He was a lot further out now and he could barely hear his brother.

Harry knew the game his brother was talking about. It was Beckham's sensational winning free kick against Greece that had sealed England's qualification for the 2002 World Cup. Harry remembered the reactions to the goal in his own house and in the stadium. He couldn't imagine scoring a goal that meant that much to people.

Even so, now he began to imagine it was him. It was Harry Kane taking the free kick against Greece, wearing the number 7 shirt for England, with the captain's armband around his arm.

Harry placed the ball and took a few steps back, copying Beckham. He took a deep breath and looked from the ball to the goal where Charlie now stood. He raised a hand to shield his eyes against the sun.

Then he charged forward, imagining the commentary in his head as he wrapped his right foot around the ball, looking to curl it towards the top corner.

The ball rose a few inches off the ground, but quickly came back down again and rolled softly into Charlie's arms. His brother hadn't even needed to dive.

Harry kicked the ground in annoyance. It was a good thing there hadn't been a crowd – he'd have been booed off for that one.

"OK, maybe you should be a *bit* closer!" Charlie laughed, rolling the ball back towards Harry.

"No!" Harry shouted. "Let me have another go!"

He was determined to keep trying until he got it right, even if they were there all night. Once he'd set his mind on something, he wasn't going to stop until he had it perfected.

The next kick flew off to the right. The one after that didn't even get off the ground. The next went over the bar. But Harry kept going. Ten more, twenty more, a hundred more …

When they eventually hoisted the goal back over the fence and into their garden, he'd only done it "perfectly" (by his standards) a couple of times. But Harry knew this wouldn't be the last time he was out there. Tomorrow night he'd be back, making Charlie stand in goal as he peppered him with more shots.

"So how long do you think he's going to stay?" Katie asked, passing the ball to Harry. Katie was one of Harry's best friends at school, loving football almost as much as he did.

"I don't know," he replied, as he passed the ball back

to her. "He's probably just going to take some pictures and leave. Hopefully at least we'll get to meet him."

Harry's morning Maths and History lessons flew by. He was soon out on the field at break-time, kicking a ball about with his friends.

Katie swung in a cross towards Harry, and he imagined he was at the World Cup and it was Beckham who'd played the pass. Harry ran across the face of the goal and smashed the ball into the net with a bullet header.

"There he is!" Katie suddenly shouted, pointing across the school field. Everyone stopped playing and turned in disbelief. David Beckham was standing right there in the car park!

Harry thought he was dreaming.

They all ran to the assembly hall, where David was due to speak in front of the whole school. They watched and listened in awe as he talked about Chingford, about playing for Manchester United and his time as England captain.

After his talk, David made his way around the hall to chat with some of the students. Only one thing was going through Harry's mind as David approached. *Please pick me. Please pick me.*

"What's your name, kid?" David asked, looking straight at Harry.

"Harry Kane," he replied, his voice quivering. Then he worked up the courage to say the one thing he really wanted to tell his hero.

"I'm going to be the England captain one day."

A few students nearby laughed quietly, but Harry only cared about one other person's opinion.

"Really?" Beckham said with a grin. "If you work hard, anything is possible. Good luck, mate."

And with that, he was gone.

Harry watched Beckham as he moved on to talk to some of the other students. Harry's chest felt warm and fuzzy. Maybe *he'd* be back at Chingford one day, inspiring the next generation.

Now Harry felt more determined than ever. One day, he *was* going to be England captain.

# 3

## STEPPING STONE

*Late 2004, Watford Youth Academy, Watford, England*

"Watford are a decent team," Harry's dad said encouragingly. "You'll develop there if you work hard – then you can move on to a bigger club in a few years."

Harry wasn't sure. It was true that many of the top players had started their careers at smaller clubs like Watford, but Harry had already failed trials at both Arsenal and Tottenham. Only Watford had taken him.

"But what if I'm just not good enough for the top clubs?" Harry asked, looking up at his dad. Watford wasn't where he wanted to be, and it just didn't feel permanent.

"If you quit now, you'll never know," his dad replied. "You've *got* to believe in yourself, Harry."

Harry couldn't help but wonder whether football was right for him. He'd been so determined to become a professional footballer, to go all the way to the top and captain England, but at the moment that dream felt further away than ever.

Thinking back, he almost felt embarrassed about what he'd said to David Beckham earlier in the year, about being the England captain. If Harry wasn't going to make it to the top, part of him just wanted to go back to Ridgeway Rovers, his local team, and focus on school.

"You're only eleven, Harry," his dad continued. "It would be daft to give it all up now. Why don't you give it a go at Watford, even if it's only for a few weeks?"

Memories of what David Beckham had said to Harry came back to him. *If you work hard, anything is possible.*

"You're right, Dad. I'll give it a go."

Beckham's words were a new source of motivation for Harry. If it was going to happen, he'd need to work hard.

Perhaps Watford really were the perfect stepping-stone for Harry to go all the way to the top.

# 4

## MOVING UP

*Late 2004, Watford, England*
*Watford Academy v Tottenham Hotspur Academy*

"Yes, Harry! Go on, son!" his dad shouted.

The crowd was small, but to Harry it was loud enough to feel like a full stadium. It was only a youth game, but every player out on the pitch was there to prove themselves.

Watford were playing Tottenham, one of the teams Harry had trialled with and been rejected from. But today his skills on the ball were really shining through. Playing in his favourite central-midfield position, he was able to get a lot of the ball and control the game with his passing and dribbling.

Harry was elusive, twisting and turning with the ball past the defenders. He could read the game more quickly than anyone else, and the Spurs players couldn't get near him.

"That's class, H, well done!" his dad cheered again. Like most of his friends, Harry's parents often called Harry by his nickname.

Harry was glad his dad had convinced him to give it a go at Watford. He'd become one of the best players in the team, despite being one of the smallest.

Late in the second half, Harry burst into space between two Tottenham midfielders on the edge of the box.

"Yes! Now!" he cried to his team-mate, who was out on the wing with the ball.

Harry delicately controlled the pass, before unleashing a curling effort that dipped into the far corner of the goal. His team-mates all jumped on top of him as the home crowd cheered. Harry had capped off a Man of the Match performance with a goal, giving Watford a 3-0 victory.

"I can go all the way to the top if I keep playing like this," Harry muttered to himself.

He wasn't the only one who was thinking that. At the end of the game, Harry noticed one of the Spurs coaches approaching his dad on the sidelines. At his trial with them, Spurs had told him he was too small. Were they now changing their mind?

Harry watched his dad shake hands with the Tottenham coach and then run over to him.

"Spurs want to sign you, Harry!" he said, giving his son a big hug. "Can you believe it? You proved yourself today, mate. I'm so proud of you!"

Harry just stood there, a huge grin on his face. He was going to play for the club that both his dad and his brother supported. It was a dream come true for the whole family.

And Harry's dream of becoming England captain was now one step closer.

# 5

# GOOD ADVICE

*Late 2005, Hotspur Way Training Ground, London, England*

"Look, he's not strong and he's not quick," one of the coaches began. "I just can't see where he fits in."

"Yeah, but he works hard," the other replied.

"Is that enough?"

"He's only young. Give him time and I'm sure he'll grow into his body, while he works on the other aspects of his game."

Harry could see the coaches glancing over at him. He knew they were talking about him.

His career at Spurs had barely begun, but already he was being held back by something he could do nothing about – his size. Most of the other boys there were already much bigger and stronger than he was.

Harry could dominate at Watford despite being small, but doing the same at Tottenham was a lot harder – the standard was so much higher here than at Watford.

He barely played in most of the teams at Spurs, spending a lot of his time as a substitute, watching the other players from the bench.

"Who cares about size, bro?" his brother Charlie laughed. "Look at Defoe this season. He's been scoring loads of goals – and he's tiny!"

"Yeah, but he's quick," Harry shot back. "I don't have that speed."

"True, but look at Teddy Sheringham," his dad interrupted.

"What about him?" asked Harry.

"He wasn't amazingly quick, or big and strong, but

27

he was always in the right place at the right time to score goals. There's loads of players who've been in a similar situation to you and have made it. You're going to grow, H, but it might just take you a bit longer than the others. In fact, if you think about it, it's kind of an opportunity."

Harry looked at him, confused.

"Because you've got to where you are without being tall, you can't rely on your pace or your strength. That gives you the opportunity to be better than the others at everything else – your touch, your passing, your shooting. Then, when you do grow, you'll have an advantage over everyone else."

Harry hadn't thought about it this way before. He glanced at Charlie, who smiled and nodded.

Harry spent the next year working harder than any of the other players at Spurs. He was still the smallest, but the coaches noticed his efforts – and soon he was improving more quickly than any of his team-mates.

His time with Charlie back in Ridgeway Park in

North London, behind their house, was also proving to be time well spent.

Now he was that bit older, Harry had more training time at Spurs than he'd had at Watford, meaning he could practise free kicks at the end of every session. Before long, he'd built on his practice with Charlie to become the best free-kick taker in the Spurs Academy squad.

Slowly but surely, Harry's playing time increased – until he was so good that the coaches simply looked past his height.

Harry had grown from benchwarmer into being the first name on the team sheet.

# 6
## SHOOTING PRACTICE

*July 2008, Hotspur Way Training Ground, London, England*

"You were one of my heroes when I was younger," Harry told Jermain Defoe as they warmed up for a shooting drill. "I used to spend hours watching videos of you on YouTube."

"You're making me feel ancient, Harry!" Jermain laughed.

As his dad had predicted, Harry's growth spurt

eventually did happen and he'd grown several inches. His position on the pitch had changed too. His shooting skills had impressed the coaching staff so much that they'd decided to move him further up the pitch, to give him more goalscoring opportunities.

Harry was now the hotshot young striker in the Spurs Academy, and there were whispers that he might start training with the first team soon. That's why he was training today with Defoe, one of Tottenham's most experienced and important strikers.

Harry watched Jermain as he snaked in and out of the cones, before accurately placing a shot from outside the box right in the top corner.

"How'd you get to be so accurate with so much power?" Harry asked, as Jermain jogged back towards him.

"Getting the power is the easy bit," Jermain replied. "For *you* it will be anyway – you're much bigger than me!" Harry smiled, thinking about how he used to be the small one. "It's the accuracy that's hard. Picking your spot and finding it," Jermain continued.

Harry was up next in the drill. He skipped round the

cones, before blasting a shot towards goal. The ball flew at some pace, but was way over the bar. Harry was baffled.

"Well, you definitely don't need to worry about power!" Jermain chuckled. "But maybe we should work on your accuracy a little bit."

"I don't know if I can do both," Harry admitted, shaking his head.

"You can and you will," Jermain told him. "You've been playing for, what, ten years? I've been playing for double that! I struggled just as much as you at your age, probably even more! I mean, if it was easy, every player would be great at shooting."

Jermain was right, but Harry knew it was a different world back when Jermain had come through the Academy. Now, if Harry wasn't up to scratch, Spurs could use their extensive scouting network and just buy a new striker who was ready for senior football.

"Look, let's do a few more of these sessions," Jermain offered, putting his arm around Harry's shoulder. "It'll be good for me as well, and the lads say you're always up for an extra session or two."

"Always!" said Harry eagerly.

"Cool. In that case, here's a tip for you right now," Jermain said. "Remember to keep your head over the ball. It stops you from leaning back and kicking it high, as if you're playing rugby!"

Harry nodded, annoyed to have forgotten such basic advice. It was something every player was taught at a young age, but he rarely thought about it when shooting during a match.

"I know it's more exciting when you smash one into the top corner," Jermain continued, "but most goals aren't like that. Most goals are scrappy, but they get you on the scoresheet."

"Your goals always seem quite nice to me," Harry admitted.

"Those are just the ones you remember," Jermain assured him. "One more thing I'd recommend. Always aim *across* the keeper and go for the far post. No keeper wants to be beaten at their near post, so they always keep that one covered. The far side is where the space is."

Following Jermain's advice, Harry's first few shots either missed the target or were comfortably saved by the keeper, just as when Harry first began practising free kicks. It was only at the end of the session that he started to score a few.

"It'll take time, H," Jermain said, starting to pack up the cones. "Don't expect it to come straight away."

"Leave the cones," Harry replied. "I want to try a few more."

Jermain raised an eyebrow, grinned and wandered back inside.

There wasn't a goalkeeper any more – just Harry and the goal. More and more shots fizzed into the back of the net as Harry kept practising. He knew that, even if there *had* been a goalkeeper, he wouldn't be stopping any of these.

By the time he'd finished, an hour after Jermain had left, it was starting to get dark. Harry picked up the cones and headed inside to wind down with some physio, a shower and food.

"What are you so happy about?" asked one of the coaches still at the training ground.

"You'll find out in our next match."

# 7

## TRUST

*August 2011, Hotspur Way Training Ground, London, England*

"Look, H, you had a good spell at Orient. I caught some of the games and your movement impressed me. You've got a lot of potential." Harry was talking to Spurs manager Harry Redknapp.

Harry had improved hugely, but he wasn't yet ready for the first team, so he'd been sent on loan to Leyton Orient in League One for the second half of last season.

It had given him match experience at a lower level than the Premier League.

This had made sense to Harry – he wanted to be playing competitive matches every week and developing as much as possible, especially after seeing some of his team-mates from the Academy, such as Ryan Mason, getting loan opportunities and thriving. But he'd often found himself on the bench at Leyton Orient, scoring "only" five goals in 18 matches.

"I want you with us this season," Redknapp continued, "at least for the first part."

Harry looked up in excitement.

"So you don't need to worry about other clubs at the moment," the manager continued. "Trust me, we've had a lot of interest. I'm not the only one who's been impressed by your performances at Orient."

Harry had been worrying over the summer that Spurs might want to sell him if he couldn't get into the Leyton Orient team, but it was a relief to hear that Redknapp was impressed, despite Harry's limited playing time.

"We're in the Europa League this year. We're going to need the full depth of our squad, because we've lost

Crouchy and there's a striker spot up for grabs. So you're going to be our guy for the European games."

Harry was the fourth or fifth choice striker, but here was Redknapp guaranteeing him a first-team debut against European opponents – a level far above anything he'd played in before.

The first thing Harry did was tell his dad and brother.

"I can't believe my boy is going to be playing for my team. It's brilliant, H!" his dad exclaimed.

"You'll need to do well, so you get to be on TV more than once," Charlie added sarcastically.

"Come on, Charlie," Harry's dad remarked. "We both know Harry will end up playing more than one game."

Harry didn't know what to say. His family were so excited for him, but he was already imagining his first game and everything that would happen if he scored.

He closed his eyes, picturing himself celebrating in front of a packed White Hart Lane, with the fans cheering his name.

Harry didn't know it, but he was grinning from ear to ear.

# 8

# THE LOWEST LOW

*August 2011, White Hart Lane, London, England*
*Europa League Qualifying, Spurs v Hearts*

"Stick with me, Harry," urged Roman as he turned to face him in the tunnel. "Let me do the dirty work. You get out there and get a goal or two. The crowd will go crazy."

The season had only just begun, but Harry's big moment had already arrived. Spurs had won 5-0 away against Hearts in the first leg of a qualifying game for the Europa League, meaning that the pressure would be off for the second leg. Redknapp had decided to give a few youth players some first-team experience, so Harry was starting up front alongside the experienced Russian striker, Roman Pavlyuchenko.

With Spurs' five-goal advantage, the home crowd were in a carefree mood, but Harry decided to play as if it was 0-0. It was his big chance to prove himself, and it would be the icing on the cake if he could bag any goals.

His opportunity came half an hour in. Fellow youth player Tom Carroll slipped a ball in behind the defence and Harry chased after it, desperate to get a touch ahead of the Hearts defender.

Harry got there first and knocked it past the keeper, but the goalie's arms flew into Harry's shins. Harry lost his balance and tumbled over.

By the time he'd turned to appeal for a penalty, the referee had already given it. Setting up a penalty was the dream start to his Tottenham career, but it was about to get even better.

"You take it, Harry," Pavlyuchenko told him, grabbing the ball and giving it to him.

"Go on, H!" Tom Huddlestone shouted, clapping in encouragement.

Harry couldn't believe it. It hadn't occurred to him before the game that he might be taking a penalty.

There was a large section of Hearts fans behind the goal and they were all screaming and waving at Harry, trying to put him off.

Harry's heart rate quickened and he suddenly felt very nervous. He took a deep breath as he placed the ball on the spot, trying to ignore the pressure.

He ran forward, stuttering slightly before striking the ball, aiming for the top-left corner. The ball flew towards the left side of the goal, but as soon as he'd kicked it he knew it wasn't accurate enough.

The keeper guessed the right direction and palmed the ball away. All the Hearts fans were jeering and laughing at Harry.

"Don't worry about it, H," Tom said, patting him on the back.

But Harry couldn't reply as he felt his heart sinking in his chest.

His moment had come and gone.

# 9
# THE HIGHEST HIGH

*December 2011, Tallaght Stadium, Dublin, Ireland*
*Europa League Group Stage, Shamrock Rovers v Spurs*

"You're still thinking about that penalty, aren't you?" Jermain said to Harry in the changing room.

Harry shook his head, but Jermain knew him too well. Harry had struggled to move on from that penalty miss against Hearts. In the months since, he'd only been on the bench a couple of times in the Premier League and he was yet to make an appearance.

_ure for a striker, H, is goals," Jermain
'You're like me. You're hungry for it. Trust
_y will come."

Today, Spurs were playing their last Europa League group stage game, away against Shamrock Rovers. With knockout stage qualification on the line, they were starting a strong team – meaning that Harry was on the bench yet again.

Despite the hostile Irish crowd, Spurs overwhelmed the hosts and raced into a 3-0 lead.

The scoreline remained the same well into the second half, and Harry was beginning to worry that he wasn't going to see any game-time. But then, with 15 minutes left, Redknapp turned to him.

"H! Get warmed up. You're going on."

Harry stripped off his tracksuit and stood next to the fourth official, waiting impatiently to be subbed on.

"Forget the penalty miss, Harry," Redknapp told him. "Pressure's off today. Go and get your first Spurs goal – you deserve it."

On the pitch, it was almost as if Harry was trying too hard, making too many runs and moving out of position too often. Harry felt the pressure mounting as time ticked on – he *had* to score.

"Just relax, mate," South African team-mate Steven Pienaar told him when the ball went out of play. "Don't overthink it – just play your game."

Harry took the advice and settled into his game. The Shamrock defenders kept losing track of his off-ball movement but, just as Harry was starting to feel confident, they were into the 90th minute.

Then Pienaar played the ball out wide to Danny Rose, who took one touch and floated the ball across the penalty area to Andros Townsend at the far post. The winger headed it down and the Shamrock defenders scrambled to clear it.

But Harry was one step ahead of them.

Townsend's header bounced right in front of Harry, who instinctively struck the ball towards goal. It beat both the keeper and a Shamrock defender on the goal line.

GOAL!

Harry had scored his first first-team goal – he'd gone out and got one, just as Redknapp had asked him to.

"Told you, bro!" Pienaar said with a grin, as Harry's team-mates joined him to celebrate.

The goal didn't mean anything for the result, but the away fans behind the goal were all celebrating for Harry. They knew how big a moment this was for his confidence and his career.

A weight had been lifted from Harry's shoulders. With his first Spurs goal and with a new-found confidence, he was sure it would be the first of many.

# 10

# A BETTER CHANCE

*December 2011, Hotspur Way Training Ground, London,*
*England*

"There's two types of centre-back," said Emmanuel Adebayor. "There's your big, strong, good-in-the-air types, and then there's your quick, small, but good-on-the-ball types."

"Which one is easier?" Harry asked.

"Both." Adebayor grinned.

Despite Harry's lack of playing time, he kept his head

down and continued working hard on the training pitch. Much like the centre-backs Adebayor was talking about, Harry was taller – a different kind of player to Jermain Defoe. Emmanuel was a more physical striker, more powerful in the air, and there were different things Harry could learn from him.

"When the ball is going forward, you get close to the small centre-back. You knock him around, make sure he's the one marking you at corners," Adebayor told Harry.

"And the other one?"

"If a ball is played through, or you're running with the ball, you go at him. When he has the ball, you close him down – he won't want it."

"So you know which one is which?" Harry asked.

"Of course," Adebayor replied. "Rio and Vidic, Terry and Carvalho – all the big partnerships have one of each."

Between Adebayor and Defoe, Harry was learning all the tips and tricks of how to be a complete striker, but he still craved first-team football. He'd had a small taste of it so far, but he wanted more.

He wasn't the only one feeling that way. Ryan Mason had returned from his loan spell at Doncaster Rovers and he too was itching to get back to playing, after sitting on the bench for a few games at Spurs.

"It's not the same out here on the training pitch," Ryan moaned. "We need to be going up against proper professionals, battling for three points to learn what we really need to know to get better."

"The gaffer knows what he's doing," Harry replied. Redknapp had seen Harry's potential and Harry trusted the manager to do the right thing for his career.

Then, at that very moment, Harry noticed the boss marching across the training ground towards them both.

"Ryan! H!" Redknapp shouted, beckoning them over. "How do you two fancy going out on loan again?"

The two players exchanged glances, hiding their smiles at the coincidence.

"Yeah ... " they both said, a little hesitantly.

"Millwall. In the Championship," Redknapp continued. "It's a level above your previous loan spells, and they want both of you. So pack your bags. Don't let them get relegated."

With that, Redknapp was gone and Harry and Ryan were on their way to Millwall – and first-team football.

# II
# MAKING AN IMPACT

*April 2012, The Den, London, England*
*Millwall v Leicester City*

"Just keep doing what you're doing," Jackett told him.

"What do you mean?" Harry asked. He couldn't believe the manager was so calm.

His time at Millwall hadn't started well. They were losing most of their matches and Harry felt as if he wasn't making much of an impact on the team.

He felt sure he was going to be dropped from the

starting eleven – until the manager, Kenny Jackett, reassured him.

"I can see you're frustrated," Jackett told him. "You think you don't belong here."

"I'm not scoring," Harry replied, staring at the floor. "I'm a striker. I'm supposed to score."

"That's not all a striker is, Harry," Jackett said. "You cause problems for defenders, make them work, create chances. It's so much more than just scoring goals."

"But I'm not sure I'm even doing that," Harry moaned. "We're not scoring goals or winning games."

"It'll come in time," Jackett continued. "Be patient."

It meant a lot to Harry that Jackett believed in him. His position in the starting line-up was under pressure, but the manager just wanted Harry to believe in himself.

And it worked.

Harry scored in the next match, a 3-1 victory against Burnley, and went on to score four goals in the next nine games. He even heard rumours that he was going to be part of Tottenham's first-team squad next season.

Thanks to Harry's run of goals, Millwall's results gradually improved. With just one month of the season to go, Millwall needed a win against Leicester to secure their survival in the division for another season.

Harry was starting the game up front, alongside veteran striker Andy Keogh.

"The centre-backs are both big guys, H, so they won't like it if you run at them or try and get in behind. Just avoid a physical battle," Keogh told him.

"Yeah, I've got it," Harry said confidently. It was pretty much the same advice Emmanuel Adebayor had given him back at Spurs.

After 25 minutes, a free kick from James Henry was looped high over to the far side of the box. Keogh managed to get on the end of it and headed it back across goal.

Harry drifted away from his marker, avoiding the big, powerful centre-backs. Controlling the ball delicately, he spun and blasted it into the top corner.

"Yes, H!" Keogh roared.

Harry wheeled away towards the corner flag to knee-slide in front of the triumphant home fans. Everyone knew how crucial that goal could be in avoiding relegation, and it was Harry's third game in a row where he'd scored, bringing his recent tally to five goals in 10 matches.

Later in the game, Harry darted in behind the big central defenders, following Adebayor and Keogh's advice, to latch on to a through ball.

He beat the offside trap and was through on goal but, just as he was about to unleash his shot, a Leicester defender who'd been trying to catch up with Harry clattered into the back of him. Harry fell to the ground and Millwall were given a penalty.

Andy Keogh stepped up and coolly converted. Millwall were 2-0 up, and the fans could start thinking about life in the Championship for another season.

Leicester tried to fight back late in the game and scored in the 82nd minute, but it was too late then for them to get another.

The three points – and Championship survival – were secure, and Harry had been at the centre of it. He'd only been at the club for half the season, but his goals had made such an impact that he was named Millwall's Young Player of the Year for 2011–12.

Harry was only 18, but now he knew for sure that he was going to make it at Spurs.

They couldn't ignore him now.

# 12

## ON THE MOVE

*August 2012, St. James' Park, Newcastle, England*
*Newcastle United v Spurs*

"We need a goal, Harry. Go and get one," declared the
manager, as Harry prepared to go on.

Harry had earned greater respect at Spurs after his
loan spell at Millwall. The rumours turned out to be true
and he'd found himself in the Spurs first-team squad for
the start of the new season.

There was also a new manager in charge, with André

Villas-Boas brought in to replace the sacked Harry Redknapp.

Harry was part of the match-day squad for the opening game of the season, away at Newcastle, starting on the bench.

After Spurs went 2-1 down late in the game, Harry was called over by his new boss. Harry was going to make his Premier League debut.

The Premier League was a very different experience to the Europa League games Harry had previously played in. There were over 50,000 fans inside St James' Park, and they all hissed and booed when Harry came onto the pitch.

Harry was playing up front alongside Gareth Bale and Jermain Defoe. Now there were higher demands on him than ever before.

"Harry, now!" Gareth shouted over the noise of the crowd, as he lifted a ball towards Harry. Harry sprinted after it, but he was too slow to reach it, beaten by a Newcastle defender.

Harry put his hands on his knees, panting hard. He'd only been on the pitch for a few minutes, but he was already out of breath with the tempo of the Premier League.

"Harry, get back in position!" Jermain bellowed, as he gestured Harry to move back.

The game was exhausting – brutal, in fact – and Harry struggled to contribute much to the team's efforts. But it was the Premier League. It was where he wanted to be.

Harry was improving all the time, but although he was part of the first-team squad, he wasn't quite ready to enter the starting line-up. Most of his playing time at Spurs was probably still going to be with the under-21s.

But Harry's growing reputation, after his performances at Leyton Orient and Millwall, had attracted attention from a number of clubs, desperate to get him on loan.

In the week after the Newcastle game, Tim Sherwood, manager of the under-21 team, approached Harry at the end of a training session.

"Chris Hughton wants you down at Norwich," he

said. "They're a Prem team, so it's another step up for you, but I think you're ready for it and we believe in you. If all goes well, the first team is waiting for you when you get back."

Harry was excited to have a first-team opportunity in the Premier League, but one thing concerned him.

He was a Londoner, born and bred, playing for a London club. He'd never lived outside London, but now he'd be moving away to a new city to play with established Premier League players, all fighting for Norwich to stay in the top division.

Harry was looking forward to it, but there was a lot to feel nervous about.

# 13
## LOST

*September 2012, Carrow Road, Norwich, England*
*Norwich City v Doncaster Rovers*

"You're going up front with Steve," Chris Hughton told Harry on the sidelines. "They're not the quickest, so see if you can cause them some problems."

Harry's first opportunity to prove himself to the Norwich fans arrived straight away. They had a home game against West Ham in the Premier League and, with the game deadlocked at 0-0 and 20 minutes left,

Harry was called on, playing alongside Steve Morison.

It wasn't as fast-paced as the Spurs game against Newcastle that he'd been involved in a couple of weeks earlier, but Harry still had to think a lot quicker than he'd been doing at Millwall.

With just five minutes left in the game, Harry was played in by winger Robert Snodgrass. As he dribbled towards the keeper, Harry knew that this was the perfect moment to make his mark.

He tried to drive through the ball with his left foot, imagining it flying into the top-left corner. But Harry didn't connect cleanly and, when he did look up, it was only to watch the ball roll tamely into the arms of the keeper.

Harry turned and saw the Norwich staff and players with their heads in their hands as the crowd sighed with disappointment. He'd let them all down.

Harry felt so disappointed that he didn't expect to play in Norwich's next match, three days later. But Chris Hughton trusted Harry to bounce back and had him down to start.

It was a League Cup game against Doncaster Rovers.

Harry got off to a good start, setting-up Norwich's first goal within half an hour by laying the ball off to midfielder Alex Tettey.

"You've been great, Harry," the boss told him in the dressing room at half-time. "You're causing them all kinds of problems. Just carry on doing what you're doing and I'm sure you'll get a goal in the second half."

The second half saw Harry go straight into the thick of the action, doing everything right to bounce back from the West Ham game. But the only thing still missing from his performance was a goal.

Then, only five minutes later, everything came crashing down.

Harry burst into the box to latch onto a cross, but he misjudged the flight of the ball, swinging his foot and kicking the ground. The pain was instant and he knew something was wrong. He slumped to the floor, clutching at his right foot.

Harry knew that, for him, this match was over. The big question was, how long would he be out for?

The answer was eight weeks. Harry had broken the fifth metatarsal bone in his right foot.

Even though he'd really only just arrived at the club, Harry had been struggling at Norwich. Despite the manager's support, he'd found it hard to fit in with the rest of the squad, who were a tight-knit group.

Now that he was injured, he was even more isolated.

Harry also felt completely cut off from his family and friends back in London.

"I just don't think anyone here likes me," he told his dad over the phone.

"Well, you've just got to recover from your injury and then prove yourself on the pitch," his dad reassured him. "Remember – they believe in you at Spurs. They'll want you in the first team eventually."

Harry knew his dad was right – he always talked a lot of sense.

Harry always knew there would be ups and downs throughout his career. For the moment, he just needed to ride it out.

# 14

## ANOTHER ONE

*February 2013, Hotspur Way Training Ground, London, England*

"I know it didn't go so well for you at Norwich, and I know the injury was a big part of that," Tim Sherwood told Harry.

Harry had returned to Norwich after his injury in December, but then Spurs had recalled him in the January transfer window.

Luck just hadn't gone his way at Norwich. Harry had

wanted more time to prove himself and to win his place back in the starting line-up but, once again, he put his faith in Tottenham to know what was best for him.

But then, only 20 days after being recalled by Spurs, they were loaning him out again.

"Leicester are a good team," Sherwood told him. "They're fighting for promotion in the Championship. It will be a brilliant opportunity for you – maybe even better than Norwich, although Leicester are in the division below."

Harry nodded, but he didn't agree. He'd already played in the Championship, with Millwall – now he wanted to stay in the Premier League.

He knew that going out on loan was what he needed to gain experience, but it was happening so often now that his future at Spurs was beginning to feel very uncertain.

On top of that, he was moving outside London again, after only just rejoining his friends and family back in his home city.

His worries weren't helped when he spoke to Ryan Mason, who was now out on loan in France, with FC Lorient.

"It's been a nightmare, H," Ryan told him. "I've only managed to play for the B team."

"What does Villas-Boas think?" Harry asked.

"I haven't heard from him," Mason replied, sounding gloomy. "He doesn't seem too bothered."

Harry was worried. All through his three previous loans, the one thing that had kept him going was knowing that the people at Spurs were keeping an eye on him, knowing that they had a plan for him.

But maybe there was no plan. Maybe he just didn't matter any more.

# 15

# STICK OR TWIST?

*July 2013, Hotspur Way Training Ground, London, England*

"Trust me, Harry," said Ryan, as they walked off the training pitch. "This year will be better. This year we're going to make our mark."

"I hope you're right," replied Harry, taking a deep breath. "This season's going to be different. It has to be."

Harry had played for three different clubs in the previous season, but had only started in eight games, scoring just two goals. He'd scored in his home debut for Leicester, as part of a 3-0 win against Blackburn Rovers, but he'd seen very little game time after that.

He'd thought it would be the season leading him directly to the Tottenham first team, but in fact it had been the worst season of his senior career so far.

He wasn't even sure he'd done enough for Spurs to keep him around.

Just last week, Harry had talked to his dad about it all.

"How am I supposed to make it at Spurs if I can't even get in the Leicester team in the Championship?" Harry had asked.

"Nobody goes straight into the first team," his dad had said. "Remember, H, it's never a straight line to the top. There's going to be setbacks."

"But I'm 20 this summer! I can't do another Championship loan – people are going to think I'm not good enough for the Premier League."

"If you don't like Spurs' plans for you, H, you can always look for a move elsewhere. But I don't think you need to be thinking about that yet."

Harry hadn't replied. He'd always convinced himself that leaving Spurs permanently wasn't an option, but he knew there'd need to be a conversation about that soon.

Back in the changing room, Tim Sherwood came up to Harry.

"They want you to stay here this year, Harry," Sherwood said, smiling. He could see that Harry had been expecting him to say the opposite.

"Seriously?" Harry exclaimed.

"The manager sees you as a third or fourth choice striker, at least 'til January. You're moving up the pecking order, mate!"

Harry thought that was a strange decision, after not playing much for Leicester, but he was thankful that Spurs were willing to stick with him. He still hadn't talked much with Spurs' first team manager, André Villas-Boas, even after his Premier League debut against Newcastle last year.

But Harry knew for sure that if he could prove himself to Villas-Boas, he'd be able to break into the first team – at the only club he'd ever wanted to play for.

# 16
## LIFT-OFF

*April 2014, White Hart Lane, London, England*
*Tottenham Hotspur v Sunderland*

"You're going up front with Adebayor," Sherwood told him. "You've been decent from the bench, H, but I think you're ready for more playing time. Emmanuel will handle the defenders and give you space."

Harry's relationship with Villas-Boas hadn't improved, but then, only a few months into the new season, poor results had led to Villas-Boas being sacked.

Tim Sherwood had replaced him as first-team manager, which suited Harry very well. He and Sherwood already knew each other well and Harry was confident he'd be given more chances by the new manager.

After a few subs, Sherwood finally gave Harry his first Premier League start in a home match against Sunderland, towards the end of the season.

It was Harry's first start at White Hart Lane since the Hearts game, three years ago, when he'd missed that penalty. But Harry was a different player now – more rounded, more mature.

As the players walked out onto the pitch in front of the excited home fans, the noise of the crowd didn't make Harry nervous. Rather, it just made him more confident.

Sunderland took a surprise early lead, but Adebayor quickly levelled things up, guiding a Christian Eriksen cross into the back of the net.

Harry had struggled to get a foothold in the game and he expected to be taken off at half-time, but Sherwood kept him on.

"I know it's been difficult, H, but I'm encouraged by what I'm seeing from you," he said. "Keep working hard. I'll be leaving you on for another 30 minutes at least, so you're going to have plenty of time."

Harry appreciated Sherwood's faith in him and wanted to repay that faith with a goal.

On the hour mark, Eriksen picked the ball up on the left side of the box. He cut inside onto his stronger right foot, looking up towards the box. Harry picked up the midfielder's intentions and lurked behind the centre-backs, onside but out of sight.

The cross was perfect, bouncing through the space between the defenders, and Harry's position caught them all completely off guard.

He stuck out his right leg to put the ball into the bottom-right corner. He made decent enough contact, but expected the shot to be saved. So he was surprised to see the ball race past the keeper into the back of the net.

GOAL!

Harry wheeled away to celebrate in front of the cheering fans. His team-mates jumped on him, embracing him, all wanting to get a piece of the new kid on the block.

It was his first Premier League goal, and it was even more special for being in front of a packed White Hart Lane. It felt like his first real Tottenham goal.

"Yes, Harry!" shouted a delighted Tim Sherwood from the sidelines.

Harry was on a roll now and felt like a different player. Just after Eriksen scored Tottenham's third goal, Harry picked up the ball just outside the box, turned towards goal and skipped past a couple of defenders before unleashing a shot.

The Sunderland keeper just managed to palm it away, only for Harry's strike partner Adebayor to tap the rebound into an empty net.

"Sorry, H," he laughed. "I'm having that one."

Harry didn't mind. At last, he was feeling really at home with Spurs, and he knew for sure that his first Premier League goal was only going to be the first of many.

# 17
# NEW BOSS

*May 2014, Hotspur Way Training Ground, London, England*

"Welcome, Harry," said Mauricio Pochettino, reaching out a hand and inviting Harry into his office to sit down.

After a few bad results, Tim Sherwood had been sacked as Tottenham manager – which had left Harry feeling nervous.

Sherwood had always believed in him and had been giving him more chances in the first team. Now, with a new manager, Harry might have to prove himself all over again.

"What do we know about the new manager, then?" Harry had asked Kyle Walker and Andros Townsend. They'd both been playing regularly in the Premier League over the last couple of seasons, and he figured they might know a bit more about Pochettino.

"Not a lot," Andros shrugged.

"Southampton played some great football under him," Kyle added more positively. "He did really well with them."

"Didn't he bring a few young players through too?" Harry asked. That was his main concern right now. Sherwood had brought young Harry into the first team – he didn't want that to stop now.

"I guess," Kyle replied. "We'll have to wait and see."

Harry was sweating as he sat down in Pochettino's office.

"I'm going to be honest with you, Harry." Pochettino smiled, looking directly at his striker. "At the moment, I see you as my third choice striker, behind Soldado and Adebayor."

The new manager paused, measuring Harry's reaction. He saw the strain in Harry's face as he tried to hide his disappointment.

"However, that's not set in stone. You'll be on the bench in the league, but you'll be playing in Europe and in the cup games. If you impress me, my team can change."

Poch paused to let that sink in, then continued. "I'm saying the same thing to you as I'll say to Ryan Mason, Andros Townsend and Nabil Bentaleb. I don't care if you came through the Academy or were signed for 30 million. I judge players on their performances, not their reputations."

Hearing these words, Harry started to feel more upbeat. The disappointment of Pochettino's opening words had given way to new hope.

Harry believed the new manager when he said that he would judge players on how they played.

All Harry had to do, then, to get in the first team, was to play well. Now was the time for Harry to play his way up from third choice and into the starting eleven.

# 18
# BREAKTHROUGH

*November 2014, Villa Park, Birmingham, England*
*Aston Villa v Tottenham Hotspur*

"We need you in the team," Ryan Mason said to Harry in the dressing room.

"I don't think the boss agrees," Harry replied.

Neither Roberto Soldado nor Emmanuel Adebayor were in great form, which meant that Harry was knocking on the door of the starting line-up.

But no one seemed to be listening.

Pochettino had tried every kind of formation to get Soldado and Adebayor scoring but, so far, Harry was the only first-team striker who was getting goals. But he wasn't playing in Premier League games.

"I'm sure the boss knows he needs you, H," Ryan said. "He's just under pressure. He can't come in as the new boss and drop Soldado straight away. Not after the club paid so much for him."

"I thought he said that every player was equal," Harry scowled.

"We are, but he just needs to prove to the board that he gave Roberto a chance before giving up on him. It's just politics, H." Ryan patted Harry on the back before walking onto the pitch to warm up.

Spurs were playing away at Aston Villa and Mason was starting in centre-midfield. Up front, Pochettino had once again gone for Adebayor and Soldado, with Harry on the bench.

Villa took an early lead and for a long time it looked as if Spurs weren't going to find their way back into the match. Adebayor and Soldado missed every chance that came their way.

After another chance went begging on the hour mark, Pochettino turned towards the bench.

"Harry!" he called. "You're going on!"

It was the earliest Harry had been subbed on in a league game under Poch. There was half an hour left for Harry to prove that he belonged in the team.

The Spurs fans cheered as Harry ran on, knowing that they had a better chance with him on the pitch. Fortunately, Villa went down to 10 men soon after Harry was subbed on, and Spurs began to increase the pressure on the home team.

Spurs finally grabbed the equaliser in the 84th minute, thanks to Nacer Chadli. Then, in the last minute of the 90, Spurs won a free kick 25 yards out. This would surely be Spurs' last chance to win the game.

Harry looked around, wondering who was going to take it, but nobody stepped forward.

"I'll have it," he yelled, grabbing the ball.

"You sure?" Ryan Mason asked him, taken aback. It was a huge statement for such a young player to take control of a tense situation like this.

"Yeah," Harry said, without looking at Ryan.

There were jeers all around the stadium as he took a deep breath. That missed penalty on his Spurs debut against Hearts drifted into his mind, but he dismissed the thought and focused on the ball. There'd been so many setbacks in Harry's career so far – this wasn't going to be another.

The ref blew his whistle and Harry drew on all his extra hours of free kick practice over the years. He ran at the ball confidently, but slightly miskicked it.

The ball curled into the air, then deflected off a Villa defender's head in the wall and flew towards the centre of the goal, away from the keeper.

GOAL!

Harry sprinted over to the small section of cheering Spurs fans in the corner of the stadium. He belly-slid across the pitch in front of them, and all of Harry's team-mates followed him in celebration.

Harry had grabbed his chance in the first team with both hands by scoring a last-minute winner, and he wasn't going to let it go.

"Job done, Harry!" grinned Ryan at the final whistle. "Poch can't ignore you now!"

# 19
# DREAM DEBUT

*March 2015, Wembley, London, England*
*European Championships Qualifying, England v Lithuania*

"Harry, it's Roy. How do you fancy playing for England?"

Harry gripped the phone tightly, too shocked to reply.

"You still there, Harry?" Roy Hodgson asked.

"Yeah, yeah!" Harry said, realising he'd not said anything. "Of course. Playing for England is my dream!"

"That's good to hear. You're going to be in my squad for the games against Italy and Lithuania."

After the call, Harry's mind was a whirl of thoughts and emotions. Back in his schooldays he had told his hero that one day he was going to captain England – and now here he was, getting a foothold in the first team.

His goal of one day captaining England had just taken a huge step nearer.

Harry's first England match was against Lithuania, a qualifying game for the European Championships. England were in with a very good chance of qualifying after previous wins, but it was important to keep the momentum going.

Harry started the game on the bench alongside Ryan Mason, who'd also been called up to England's senior team for the first time. The pair followed the rest of the players out into Wembley Stadium, where 90,000 fans were eagerly awaiting their heroes.

"It makes the Lane look pathetic," Harry remarked to Ryan on the bench, awestruck by the size of the stadium.

England were on top right from kick-off. Wayne Rooney and Danny Welbeck put England into a quick 2-0 lead, and Raheem Sterling made it three early in the second half.

With England looking so comfortable, Harry felt sure he'd get the chance to go on. Sure enough, 25 minutes into the second half Rooney came off – and Harry was on.

Rooney put his arm around Harry as they swapped places on the touchline.

"Go on, H," he said excitedly into Harry's ear. "Go and get a goal!"

It meant a lot to Harry to hear such encouragement from a legend like Rooney. One day he might be doing the same to England's next generation of young strikers.

There was some applause as Harry ran onto the pitch, but many England supporters were more muted. A lot of England fans were supporters of Arsenal and Chelsea, Spurs' London rivals.

But that all changed within two minutes of Harry coming on.

Sterling picked up the ball on the left side of the box, twisting and turning past the opposition defence towards the byline. Harry could see where Raheem was looking and he pulled away from the central defenders, moving towards the far post.

"Raheem!" he called. "Over the top!"

The ball from Raheem was weighted perfectly, floating towards Harry over the Lithuanian defenders' heads. He met it with his head and directed the ball downwards.

The keeper couldn't reach down far enough to stop the ball's momentum and it went in.

GOAL!

As the ball hit the back of the net, Harry peeled away to the corner flag, soaking in the atmosphere of the crowd.

He had scored his first goal for England – just 79 seconds into his first appearance, and with his very first touch.

*That* was how to make a Wembley dream debut.

# 20
## NEW CONNECTIONS

*August 2015, Hotspur Way Training Ground, London, England*

"We had a good season, Harry," Poch told him, during a pre-season training session, "but I'm ready to make this season even better. I hope you are too."

It had been Harry's best season of his career by far. He'd finished with 31 goals for Spurs in all competitions, and had also won PFA Young Player of the Year.

But, disappointingly, Spurs had finished the league

season in fifth, missing out on both Champions League football and trophies.

But now there was a sense of optimism around the club. Pochettino had introduced a different style of football and, true to his word, he'd given opportunities to players who'd been overlooked by previous managers – and that included Harry.

Poch needed more than optimism though – he needed results to back it up.

"We're going to build the team around you," he told Harry, "and we've brought in some new faces who're going to help us do that."

Harry couldn't have heard better news. He was going to be Spurs' key player up front.

"Now, I know you stay late and get some extra training in after the team sessions, but I want you to take some of the new boys with you today and work on some movement drills," the boss added. "I want it all to be second nature when you guys get out on the pitch."

Harry enjoyed his solo drills, but it had been a while since he'd worked with another player, as he'd done with Jermain Defoe in his Academy days.

Harry knew how important it was to build chemistry within the squad. If he could create bonds with the new players that were anything like the relationship he already shared with Christian Eriksen, then he knew Spurs could be a top attacking team.

The new boys turned out to be South Korean winger Heung-min Son and young English midfielder Dele Alli.

"You want to do some extra work after the group session today?" Harry asked Son.

"Sure, great idea. Let's do it."

The pair of them stayed late with Christian – so late in fact that the floodlights had to be turned on. Eriksen fired crosses into the box and the pair of them made runs towards the near and far posts to finish them off. Then they'd swap positions.

Within hours, Harry and Son were already working together instinctively – when Harry went one way, Son would immediately go the other.

Son had the right work ethic too.

Harry couldn't wait to see how his connection with Son would work out on the pitch.

# 21
# ANSWERING THE CRITICS

*October 2015, Vitality Stadium, Bournemouth, England*
*Bournemouth v Spurs*

"Harry?" The voice came from along the corridor, then Poch's head appeared around the door. "There you are. What's going on? Why aren't you warming up with the rest of the lads?"

"I'm just trying to focus," Harry replied, sitting on his own in the changing room. "I haven't got going this season – I just need to work out what's been going wrong."

Spurs were already nine games into the League season, but Harry had only scored once and the media were already calling him a "one-season wonder".

The press were sapping Harry's confidence.

"Why does it matter what *they* think?" Harry's dad, always the voice of reason, had told him. "The only opinion that matters is Mauricio's."

"I guess ... " Harry had replied. "But ... what if they're right? What if that's all I am?"

Now Poch sat down next to Harry in the dressing room.

"Nothing's going wrong, Harry. You had an incredible season last year, but you can't expect to do that every season. Every striker goes through dry spells. What's important is that you don't lose confidence."

"I know, but sometimes it gets hard to ignore what people are saying about me."

"Let them talk. Trust me, Harry, I've seen players get lucky and have one good season. You're not one of them. With a player of your ability and work rate, you're going to be a top player for a long time. Just trust me."

Poch stood up and zipped up his tracksuit jacket.

"Now, go and get warmed up with your team-mates. You won't be replaced in this team any time soon, so no need to worry about that. Just relax and play your football. The results will come."

Poch's faith in him meant a lot to Harry. He knew he just needed to find his form and repay that faith.

The Bournemouth match got off to the worst possible start when the hosts took the lead inside the first minute.

But five minutes later, Christian Eriksen spotted Harry darting into space behind the Bournemouth defence, beating the offside trap. Christian slipped the ball through to him.

Then, before Harry could get a touch, the Bournemouth keeper clipped his ankles, bringing him down. Spurs were awarded a penalty, and there was only ever going to be one man taking it.

Harry composed himself and ran towards the ball. He slipped as he connected with it, but he'd sent the keeper the wrong way and the ball slammed into the net.

The goal was exactly the confidence boost Harry needed.

"I thought you'd missed that!" joked Dele Alli.

"Never!" Harry laughed.

Even though Spurs were 3-1 up at half-time, Harry had only scored the penalty. He wanted more goals.

Minutes into the second half, a Christian Eriksen cross was placed perfectly for Harry to attack, just the sort of ball he'd received when he'd been practising with Son on the training pitch.

Finding himself unmarked behind a Bournemouth defender at the back post, Harry stuck out his right leg to poke the ball into the back of the net. It was a classic poacher's goal.

Now Harry had two, he set his eyes on a hat-trick.

Minutes later, a Christian Eriksen corner was headed goalwards, but the shot was blocked by the keeper. The rebound fell to Harry, who stabbed it in with his right foot. As with his second goal, Harry's striker instincts had put him in the right position at the right time.

The Bournemouth crowd was stunned into silence as the Spurs players and fans all celebrated Harry's success.

He'd answered his critics in style. Spurs' star player was back, and he knew that the footballing world would take notice.

# 22

# TAKING ON THE BEST

*August 2016, Hotspur Way Training Ground, London, England*

"Why did they have you on corners and not in the box?" Jan Vertonghen asked Harry. "You would've been the most dangerous guy in there!"

"I don't know," Harry shrugged. "But it won't happen again."

Harry had just returned from a very disappointing European Championships for England, with many fans blaming some questionable decisions by Roy Hodgson for the poor performances.

Harry had had a great season after the hat-trick at Bournemouth, collecting the Golden Boot for top scorer in the league and being named in the Premier League team of the year.

He was frustrated that his form hadn't translated to the England team, but now he was back at Spurs, where Pochettino had called a team meeting.

Poch was just as clear about his ambitions for the upcoming season as he had been this time last year.

"We came close last year, lads. Only a few more points and we would have won some silverware. This year, we're going to finish above Arsenal – and we're going to win a trophy."

There was a muted reaction among the players and, as soon as Pochettino left the room, the whispers began.

"Should we really be aiming that high?" Eric Dier asked, leaning in towards Harry. "City have got Pep now, United have Mourinho. Are we *really* good enough to compete with them?"

"We can definitely get top four," Vertonghen added. "Maybe we should settle for that."

"Come on, boys," said Harry, standing up and turning towards the rest of the squad. "We've improved massively under Poch. Why would we give up now? Why settle for less? We have the skills – we just need the confidence."

Many of the players in the room looked around, uncertainty on their faces.

Harry looked straight at Heung-min Son, Dele Alli and Christian Eriksen – the three team-mates he knew he could rely on. He could see his own resolve reflected in their steely looks. His and the manager's words had made them all more determined than ever.

All four players were still young and improving and Harry knew they'd be better than ever this season.

It was time to mix it up with the top teams in the league, but Harry didn't want just to join them.

He wanted to beat them.

# 23

# THE WORLD STAGE

*June 2018, Nizhny Novgorod Stadium, Nizhny Novgorod, Russia,*
*World Cup Group Stage, England v Panama*

"Thirty goals in the Premier League, 41 in all competitions, team of the year yet again, third in the league and in semi-finals of the FA Cup!"

As he listened to his dad reeling off his achievements from last season, Harry's face gave no hint of a smile.

"No trophies," he said abruptly, shrugging his shoulders. "And I didn't even get the Golden Boot!"

"Come on, H, don't beat yourself up," his dad insisted. "You scored more goals than last season. Remember, it's a team sport. It's not all down to you!"

"I know," Harry sighed. "But I'd rather score fewer goals and win a trophy."

Most players could only dream of having a season like Harry's, but he wasn't satisfied. He wanted trophies.

"The season's not over, Harry," his dad insisted. "There's still the World Cup, your first for England. That's an opportunity to win the biggest trophy of them all."

Harry's first tournament for England, at the Euros in 2016, had ended with no goals and England had crashed out in the last 16.

This time it would be different. Roy Hodgson had been replaced as manager by Gareth Southgate, who'd made Harry's childhood dream come true by making him England captain.

Now it was up to Harry to lead by example and make the other players believe they could win the tournament.

England's first game at Russia 2018 was against Tunisia, in the city of Volgograd.

"It's really important we win this one, lads," Southgate told them.

"We set the tone for the rest of our tournament tonight, boys!" Harry added. "So let's get the job done."

England came flying out of the blocks, threatening the Tunisia goal right away. Ten minutes in, Ashley Young floated in a corner which John Stones fired towards goal with a powerful header.

The goalkeeper scrambled across to save it, but the ball fell to the feet of the England captain. It wasn't one Harry was going to miss.

England were 1-0 up.

It was the dream start, but Tunisia equalised with a penalty before half-time. England kept pushing for the winner, but it still hadn't come by the 90th minute.

Then, one final chance – a last-minute corner.

Harry's Spurs team-mate Kieran Trippier whipped in the corner, which Harry Maguire was able to head on.

The ball floated towards the back post where Harry, completely unmarked, headed it home.

Harry's England team-mates bundled on top of him to celebrate, and the England fans who'd travelled to

Russia were going wild in their corner of the stadium.

It had been a hard-fought game, tougher than England had expected. But Harry had led the team to the win, scoring both goals in the process.

The result gave England the confidence boost they needed – England's ghosts from the Euro 2016 competition were quickly forgotten.

The next game was against Panama, which on paper promised to be a far easier game than Tunisia.

Southgate was keen to ensure that England maintained their focus to bag another three points, and they made the perfect start inside ten minutes, when John Stones scored with a powerful header.

Things got even better soon after, when Jesse Lingard chased down a long ball over the top of the Panamanian defence, before being bundled over by the defender.

The referee instantly pointed to the penalty spot.

Harry stepped up, prepared himself and struck the ball.

He didn't even need to see the keeper to know it was going in. The ball flew into the top-left corner and England were 2-0 up – Harry's third goal of the tournament.

Lingard quickly added a third and John Stones bagged a brace with the fourth. England were running away with it, but Harry was desperate for more.

So when England won another penalty, the only man who was ever going to take it was the captain.

Harry aimed for the top-left corner again – and it was exactly the same result.

England were 5-0 up, and it wasn't even half-time yet. And Harry now had four goals from two games, making him the tournament's top goalscorer so far.

As the players stepped out to start the second half, Harry had one thing on his mind. Another goal.

Fifteen minutes in, Ruben Loftus-Cheek fizzed a shot towards goal from outside the box. The ball deflected off the back of Harry's heel and flew into the goal.

"Sorry Ruben, but that's mine!" Harry laughed, as the team celebrated his hat-trick.

As the final whistle blew, Harry went straight over to the ref to claim the match ball.

He was in the form of his life and, if he could keep this up, England had a great chance of winning their first World Cup for more than 50 years.

# 24

# THE BIG CHANCE

*May 2019, Wanda Metropolitano, Madrid, Spain*
*Champions League Final, Liverpool v Spurs*

"I know you must've seen the rumours, Harry," said Tottenham owner Daniel Levy, "and there's not a lot I can do if they do come in for you."

Harry had been top scorer at the World Cup and as a result his reputation had never been higher, although England had been knocked out in the semi-finals and another chance for Harry to win a trophy had gone begging.

Lifting the World Cup as captain of the winning team would have been quite a triumph – something David Beckham had never managed, but Harry was sure the opportunity would come around again.

Harry's contract at Spurs was now up for renewal, so he was meeting with owner Daniel Levy to discuss his future at the club.

There had been rumours that Real Madrid and Man United were both interested in Harry, and he was convinced that winning trophies at those clubs would be much more likely than at Spurs. So Harry was keen to hear what Levy had to say.

"There haven't been any clubs enquiring about you so far," Levy told him. "And we're prepared to offer you a new contract, Harry, with a salary that's double what you're on right now."

The money was nice – and flattering too – but it wasn't Harry's real motivation. He wanted to win trophies.

"The contract commits you to Spurs, Harry. We've been on an upward trend with Mauricio, and with you, Sonny and Dele. I promise you, we're going to be winning trophies very soon. Just imagine the feeling of winning with your boyhood club.

"And we've got the new stadium coming soon," he added.

Suddenly it was all very clear to Harry. Staying loyal to his club and winning a trophy with Spurs would be much more satisfying than winning anywhere else.

He shook Daniel Levy's hand and signed on the dotted line.

Harry started the season slowly, compared to the previous two seasons. His goalscoring improved as the season went on, but then disaster struck in a home game against Man United.

With just seconds of the match remaining, Harry suddenly felt his ankle twist and he collapsed to the floor in agony. He was stretchered off, and the medical staff only needed one look at the scan of his ankle to know the worst.

"The ankle ligament is torn, Harry," the team doctor said. "You're going to be out for at least four weeks."

Just as the season was building towards its climax – and the chance to win trophies – Harry was forced onto the sidelines. He was furious.

He had to watch Spurs get dumped out of both the FA Cup and the League Cup. They fell short in the title race too, meaning that only the Champions League remained as the team's final chance to avoid another season without trophies.

"Do you really think we can win it?" Dele Alli asked Harry, when he finally returned to training. Dele was already dreaming of glory, after Spurs had gone into a 3-0 lead in the first leg of their last sixteen tie against Borussia Dortmund.

"Stranger things have happened," Harry replied calmly. "Think about Chelsea in 2012. They struggled in other competitions, but still managed to pull it off."

Now back in the team, Harry scored in the away leg against Dortmund, clearly not having lost his form.

But because Harry was the man Spurs relied on to score goals, he was playing the full 90 minutes of every match. That meant there was a real risk of aggravating his ankle ligament, or even getting another injury.

Spurs drew Premier League champions Man City in the quarter-finals. It was a tough ask, but they'd beaten City before and Harry knew there was no reason why they couldn't do it again.

The first leg was a tense clash and when Harry went flying into a challenge against his England team-mate Fabian Delph, they took each other out, with Fabian landing on Harry's leg. Fear flashed through Harry's mind as pain shot through his leg.

Having just returned from injury, Harry was sidelined once more.

Despite being underdogs, Spurs managed to battle through against City to reach the Champions League semi-finals.

So, standing with crutches on the touchline in Amsterdam, Harry witnessed one of the greatest comebacks in European footballing history, as Lucas Moura scored a last-minute winner against Ajax to take Spurs through to the final.

Harry longed to be out on the pitch, but it was some consolation that his team-mates were stepping up and proving they were good enough to win without him.

It was a race against time for Harry to be fit in time to play in the final, and days before the match he was called into Poch's office.

"I'm going to start you in the final," Pochettino announced. "You're our best player and we're going to need you if we're going to win this."

"Are you sure?" Harry asked sceptically. "All I want is to play, but I don't think I'm fully match fit."

"Harry, at 50% fitness you're better than most strikers in the world. I know how desperate you are for a trophy, and this has been three years in the making. Give it your all!"

It was a warm spring evening in Madrid and the most important day of Harry's career so far. It was the Champions League final, against Premier League rivals – and probably favourites – Liverpool.

Walking out into the packed stadium, Harry looked over to the Tottenham fans who'd travelled to Spain to watch Spurs in their first ever European Cup Final.

He could feel that his body wasn't really ready for the match, and he was disappointed that he wouldn't be able to play at his best for the fans. But he knew that he could do no more than give it his all.

Liverpool gained a quick advantage inside two minutes, when Mo Salah scored the opening goal from the penalty spot.

Spurs gained a foothold in the match and put Liverpool under pressure, especially in the second half. Son had opportunities, Dele saw an effort saved and Eriksen fired over the bar, but none of Spurs' chances were coming Harry's way. His body just couldn't react quickly enough.

Harry could only watch helplessly from the half-way line as Divock Origi put Liverpool 2-0 ahead, gifting them the Champions League trophy.

Harry's disappointment at the whistle was overwhelming. Another trophy had evaded him, and he couldn't help thinking that the outcome would have been different if he'd been fully fit.

As he watched the Liverpool players and fans celebrate, Harry suddenly felt that the chance of winning trophies at Spurs had passed him by.

It felt like the end of an era at Tottenham Hotspur.

# 25
# THE SPECIAL ONE

*November 2019, Hotspur Way Training Ground, London,*
*England*

"I guess he had it coming," Dele Alli said, shaking his head. "I mean, the results haven't been good enough."

"Yeah, but how much of that is on him?" Harry replied. "*We're* the players. He can't take *all* the blame."

"I know, H," Dele answered, looking at Harry. "But you know how it works. The board need a scapegoat, and that's the gaffer."

Spurs' season had started poorly, with defeats against Leicester, Newcastle and Brighton, all weaker teams on paper. They were also thrashed 7-2 by Bayern Munich in the Champions League.

Harry was disheartened by the bad losses. He was one of the best strikers in the world, but his career seemed to be moving in the wrong direction.

Then the news came that Pochettino had been sacked.

"So who do you think they're going to get in?" Son asked, joining in on Harry and Dele's conversation.

"Someone on Sky Sports said Mourinho," Dele replied hesitantly.

"No way, José won't come here," Harry scoffed. "He's a defensive coach. That's not how we play."

"He'll win trophies, though," Son added.

Harry couldn't deny that. Everybody knew that Mourinho won trophies. His teams didn't play the most exciting football, but he was fantastic at grinding out results by keeping clean sheets and scoring just enough to win.

Sure enough, José Mourinho was announced as the

new Spurs manager and, before anyone could properly react, he arrived at the Hotspur Training Ground and set himself up in the manager's office.

Harry still wasn't convinced that the appointment was a good one. The team's results might improve under José, but his style of play meant that Harry would have fewer goalscoring opportunities.

Without delay, José called the players into his office, one-by-one, to discuss his plans. It was only November, but the team's poor start to the season already meant that the Premier League title had gone for another year. They would have to focus on other competitions if Harry was finally going to win a trophy.

Harry strode into José's office as soon as his name was called, eager to find out more about the new manager's plans.

Mourinho wasn't a large man – he was smaller than Harry in fact – but he dominated his office. This was a man who'd won every trophy in club football, who'd managed Cristiano Ronaldo, Frank Lampard and Zlatan Ibrahimović.

And now, he was sitting in front of Harry.

"We want a trophy," José said bluntly, skipping any introductions.

Harry didn't interrupt.

"I know you want a trophy. I'm the guy who can help you win one. I've won trophies everywhere. Stick with me and I guarantee you can get one."

There was an awkward pause before Harry spoke up.

"What's the plan for the rest of this season?" he asked.

"West Ham first," José replied instantly, referring to Tottenham's next game at the weekend. "After that, who knows? I want to win every game … " he pointed directly at Harry, who leaned back and sunk into his chair a little, " … and you're going to be at the heart of it."

José stood up and started walking around his office as he spoke.

"Every time I play Tottenham, I'm worried about Kane, about Dele, about Son. You've been very good, a lot of goals. But I think you can go further.

"Under me, you can go to the next level and explode. You just need to do what I tell you."

# 26

# SENDING A MESSAGE

*October 2020, Old Trafford, Manchester, England*
*Man United v Spurs*

"I thought we were guaranteed trophies with José – he's won everywhere else!" Son moaned. "We're playing worse now than just before Poch left."

"It takes time to build a team," Harry insisted, not sure if he believed what he was saying.

"He always does better in the second season anyway," midfielder Harry Winks added. "Second year at United, he won the Europa League and almost beat City to the title. And remember, the squad's been strengthened over the summer too."

Southampton's Pierre-Emile Højbjerg and Real Madrid's Sergio Reguilón had been brought in to reinforce José's defensive style. His faith in Harry and Son meant that he hadn't brought in any new strikers.

In fact, José had changed Son's and Harry's playing styles – for the better – after a conversation they'd had at the start of the season.

"I see a different role for you this year, Harry," José had proposed. "I've watched you in training and I think your passing skills aren't used enough."

For once, Harry completely agreed with the boss. He always knew his passing was one of his biggest strengths, ever since his time as a central midfielder in the Watford and Spurs youth teams, but he didn't get many chances to use it as a striker.

"If I move Son into the middle, he's got the pace to get on the end of your passes. If you drop deep to collect the ball and then look for him over the top, he'll finish off the chances."

It was an interesting idea. Harry's relationship with Son at Spurs had always been great, and they'd combined to net a large number of goals over the years. But, it was usually Son who provided Harry with the assists.

Spurs had a decent start to Mourinho's second season with the new set-up, but their first real test came in October, away to José's old club and Premier League rivals, Man United.

"If we win today, we send a message to the rest of the league," José announced in the dressing room. "We're not looking for top six, or top four. We want the title. Let the rest of the league know that."

"Come on, lads!" Harry added. "We know that we've got what it takes to beat them."

Perhaps some of Harry's team-mates hadn't been listening, as Spurs went behind inside two minutes. United won an early penalty, which Bruno Fernandes converted.

"We keep going, lads. We come back!" Harry roared. His words seemed to give his team-mates an extra spring in their step, and within minutes Spurs were back on level terms. A mistake at the back allowed Tanguy Ndombele to smash home.

Spurs now had all the momentum and, moments later, Harry won a free kick just inside United's half.

He moved up instantly, ready to take a quick free kick, and spotted Son's run between two defenders. Picking him out with pinpoint accuracy, a few seconds later the ball was in the back of the net.

Spurs were in front.

"I guess the boss made the right change! You'll have to set me up now," Harry teased as he and Son celebrated together.

Twenty minutes later, United were down to ten men when Anthony Martial was given a straight red. Everything seemed to be going Spurs' way.

Then United tried to play out from the back, but Harry was able to intercept a lazy pass right on the edge of the penalty area. Son burst through a gap on the left and played it back into the box.

Harry was there, and he didn't even need to look at the goal. He instinctively knew where the corner was, and neatly placed the ball past the keeper.

"Thanks for returning the favour," grinned Harry as he and Son jogged back towards the half-way line. The South Korean then added a fourth, putting Spurs 4-1 up at half-time.

Mourinho's intention had been to send a message to the rest of the league that Spurs were after the title, and when Serge Aurier made it 5-1 in the second-half, they had surely made their point.

To top it all off, Welsh left-back Ben Davies was fouled as he cut inside, winning Spurs a late penalty, which Harry stepped up and tucked away.

Harry had scored twice in the 6-1 thrashing, but he'd also been heavily involved with the other Spurs goals. José's new tactics meant that Harry's game was now expanding into all aspects of the team's play.

"What do you think of that then, H?" Son asked, as they left the pitch. "You think we can win the title?"

"I don't know," Harry shrugged as he put his arm around Son's shoulder. "But if we keep playing like that, I reckon anything can happen."

# 27
# IT'S COMING HOME

*June 2021, Wembley, London, England*
*European Championships Semi-Final, England v Denmark*

"It's been a long time since we were in a semi-final together, H," Kieran Trippier said as they sat in the Wembley dressing room.

"Well, let's make sure this time round is different to 2018," Kyle Walker added.

Harry had just won both the Golden Boot and the Playmaker Award, finishing the season with the most goals and most assists in the Premier League – a stunning achievement.

However, Mourinho had been sacked a few weeks earlier and Harry had seen another season pass by without Spurs winning a trophy.

Thankfully, the end of the club season meant that he now had another chance – at the Euros.

England had improved hugely under Gareth Southgate, following their World Cup semi-final loss, and there was serious belief amongst the players and fans alike that this time around England were good enough to go two steps further and win the trophy.

"You're starting." That was all Gareth Southgate had told the England captain before their last-sixteen match against Germany.

Harry had started the tournament poorly and hadn't looked like his usual goalscoring self.

Some pundits had blamed this on fatigue after a long season at club level, but although Southgate had plenty of options for the striker position, he wasn't going to drop the captain for England's biggest match of the tournament so far.

Raheem Sterling fired England into the lead, but Germany were dangerous and threatened to equalise many times.

The Wembley crowd were getting anxious, until Jack Grealish forced himself into the Germany box on the counter-attack. He burst forwards and fired a brilliant cross into the penalty area. Harry was there to put the ball in the net.

It was Harry's first goal of the tournament, sealing a 2-0 victory over Germany and securing England's place in the next round.

As the match ended, the Wembley crowd cheerfully sang "It's Coming Home", giving the England players an extra level of belief that, with the backing of their country, they could really go and win the whole thing.

Harry added two more goals to his tally in a 4-0 thrashing of Ukraine in the quarter-finals.

England were back at Wembley for the semi-finals, taking on Denmark. England may have been favourites, but they were wary of underrating the opposition. Any team that had reached this stage of the competition had to be taken seriously.

"We've got to be ready tonight, lads," the manager said passionately. "We're yet to concede a goal in the tournament, but don't let that make us sloppy. If we concede, we keep going. We don't change what we're doing, we don't panic. We've got the quality to score more than them and win it."

"Two years ago, at the World Cup, we went one-up and stopped playing," Harry added. "We don't do that again today."

Out on the pitch, the England players sang the national anthem as loudly as they could in front of the sold-out home crowd. The atmosphere inside Wembley was electric.

England had only ever reached a major tournament final once, in 1966. That year, they'd gone on to win the cup. Could they do it again?

As expected, it was a tense start and Harry struggled to get on the ball and use his passing skills, in the way he'd been playing under Mourinho at Spurs.

Half an hour in, Denmark won a free kick about 30

yards out. Twenty-one-year-old Mikkel Damsgaard stepped up and whipped the ball into the top corner, out of Jordan Pickford's reach.

The small section of Danish fans in the stadium erupted, leaving the English fans speechless.

"This is what we've prepared for!" Harry shouted. "Nothing changes. The goal will come."

Harry dropped from the centre-forward position to pick up the ball, instantly spotting a run by Bukayo Saka. The Arsenal winger zipped into the box and fizzed the ball across goal towards Sterling. The cross was put into a threatening area, and although it didn't reach Sterling, the ball deflected off Denmark captain Simon Kjær into his own goal.

Every England fan in the stadium was jumping up and down. The noise was deafening.

England gained the upper hand after equalising, but Denmark rallied to hold on until half-time.

Then they managed to hold on for another 45 minutes.

Extra time loomed, and Harry couldn't help but think back to 2018. England's World Cup semi-final had also gone to extra time, and then it had been Croatia who'd found the extra gear and won. He was determined that the same wasn't going to happen here.

"Remember two years ago, lads? We're gonna be the team that dominates the extra thirty minutes this time!" Harry roared as the England players huddled before the restart.

The extra period was cagey, too close to call, but both teams' players were tiring, meaning that they were more likely to make mistakes.

Deep into the second half of extra time, Sterling wriggled his way into the box, but he was bundled over by a Danish defender. The referee instantly pointed to the penalty spot, and VAR agreed.

This was Harry's moment to make everything right.

He placed the ball on the spot, spinning it round until he could see the exact position he wanted to strike it.

He breathed fully and deeply.

Harry had scored many penalties throughout his career, but none in a moment as big as this. In these few seconds, he had a country's hopes resting on his shoulders.

He stared into Schmeichel's eyes, took one more deep breath, stepped up towards the ball and struck it.

Harry's eyes followed the ball's path towards the bottom right corner, only to see that Schmeichel had guessed the right way.

Harry's heart sank as he realised that the keeper was going to save it, but Schmeichel couldn't hang on to the ball, and his save guided the ball right back to Harry. Harry couldn't make any mistakes this time – and he didn't.

Every England player and every England fan in the stadium was ecstatic as they celebrated with Harry, but the captain made sure the players didn't lose their heads.

"It's not done yet, lads!" he said firmly. "Stay focused!"

The combination of Harry's words, the home crowd's support and the experience in the England team meant that the game was only ever going to have one outcome from that point.

The ref blew the final whistle and England were in the World Cup final. The entire team and coaching staff embraced, singing "Sweet Caroline" together with the ecstatic Wembley fans.

Harry took a moment by himself to drink it all in as he celebrated. He thought back to when he'd first started playing football, and to that day when he'd met David Beckham at Chingford.

Harry had told Beckham that he was going to play for England, that he was going to be the England captain.

And here he was.

Harry was closer to winning a trophy for England than Beckham ever had been.

On top of that, Harry was closing in on Spurs', England's and the Premier League's goalscoring records. He was one of the greatest strikers in the world, and the only thing missing was that first trophy.

But Harry knew that he was going to get it eventually. He'd overcome so much to get to this stage of his career, and he was going to overcome this as well.

He wasn't done yet …

In fact, Harry still felt as if it was only the beginning.

# HOW MANY
# HAVE YOU READ?